Read All the Wonderful Books
by Cascade Canyon Room 7!

INTRODUCING...

TypePro

Tomato

A

Thea

Holden

Sammy Robinson

chocolate chip cookie

Pander

Smokey

Narrator

Dr. Tommy

Amelia

Eliza almost fell over, and when she did, I fell from her bag.

"I was thinking maybe you, my family, and I could all make a plan together," I suggested.
"What kind of plan?" Boy inquired.

One night, during the witching hour, on the first floor of the lighthouse, the letter A woke up. She had heard something. It was a THUMP!

Thea had no choice, if she wanted to change her life. She had to go inside the tree.

"I must do something," thought Holden. Just then, he saw a mouse trap...

I suddenly felt like I was shrinking, squeezing, popping out fur, turning fuzzy, and getting very, very hungry! I looked down at my hands, but they weren't hands anymore, they were FURRY PAWS!

We ran for our lives. Soon we came to an open window, but we didn't know how to get out!

Xander asked his parents if he could go above ground many times, but they always said it was too dangerous. They told him that if he went above ground he could get eaten.

"Shall we get something to eat then?" Anna asked.

"I thought I told you I had reservations about this," I scolded.
"No, you didn't. You just said it was 'an ill-advised idea,'" Xander responded with a smile.

125 bones found in Tasmania, but the bone scientists there say they still need to find the last one.

She went swimming into the dark ocean alone. Amelia saw a shadow. Suddenly, she felt scared!

Books by Cascade Canyon Room 7

TypePro and the Terrifically Terrifying Adventure

The Vegetables

The Alphabet and the Giant

The Fantastic Figure

Holden and the Secret Plan

Sammy and the Pet Store

The JFF

Xander, Holden, and the Snake

Smokey and the Mysterious Disappearance

Pranks!

Dr. Tommy and the Tasmanian Trip

Amelia the Dolphin

O Brainy Book

Cascade

Canyon

O Brainy Book

written and illustrated by Room 7

Third Edition

CASCADE CANYON SCHOOL

This book is for the third graders who read The BFG *with me for the first time back in 2012 and then encouraged me to read them more and more books by Roald Dahl.*

This project, now in its fifth year, began with their enthusiasm and continually inspires reading and writing among both children and adults.

-- Trevor Mattea
Editor, *O Brainy Book*
Room 7 Teacher, Cascade Canyon School

There's more to Cascade Canyon Room 7 than great stories...

Cascade Canyon School is a small, independent school, in Fairfax, California, serving students in Kindergarten through eighth grade. Its mission is to provide a nurturing environment where its students are valued, respected, and challenged. The school seeks to infuse its academic program with the visual and performing arts, thereby generating interdisciplinary projects that connect students with the greater community, culminate with authentic products and acts of service, and prepare students for success beyond CCS.

During spring 2018, the second and third graders of Room 7 read and discussed over ten books written by Roald Dahl. They used his children's stories to inform their understanding of the elements of fiction as well as to get a sense of his unique style and Quentin Blake's illustrations. Throughout the process, students discovered several recurring characteristics, including Dahl's use of children as protagonists and adults as antagonists, imaginative vocabulary, and inspiration taken from his own life. Students then sought to draw upon those features in their own stories, which have been published together as this anthology. In fact, its name is an allusion to a scene in Dahl's *The Witches*. Students now plan to share their work with prospective families, residents of Fairfax, libraries and schools throughout the Bay Area, and readers worldwide. They will donate half of their proceeds from copies sold to benefit the Marin County Free Library and 826 Valencia.

Learn more about Cascade Canyon School and Room 7 on their website: **www.cascadecanyon.org**

Contents

Kariana Edrington

TypePro and the Terrifically Terrifying Adventure

THE WORLD'S No. 2 STORYTELLER

illustrated by Kariana Edrington

TypePro and the Terrifically Terrifying Adventure

Kariana Edrington

TypePro and the Terrifically Terrifying Adventure

illustrated by Kariana Edrington

This book is for my family; my dear friend, Norah; and adventurers everywhere.

Bored

Hi, my name is TypePro. I am a laptop computer, originally from Texas and later brought to a school in Hawaii. When I came to this school, I was brand new. Ms. Petunia bought me, so she could start teaching her students about technology. I could tell Ms. Petunia was a fantastic teacher because everyone said she had as much energy as a jumping grasshopper. She was always telling her students about her adventures. The kids told her she was "tangytastic." That means Ms. Petunia tastes like oranges. Well, at least, I think that's what it means.

You might think my life was wonderful because I was with Ms. Petunia, and kids usually love computers and other technology, but it wasn't like that at all. I was so bored in that classroom because all of her students were first graders, and they didn't even know the basics yet. None of them even knew how to type. She wanted them to learn how to type because as adults they would need to type books, emails, and other stuff like that. I stayed in the first grade classroom and never went anywhere. It was quite disappointing.

Before Ms. Petunia bought me, I was in a store with other computers. We were all friends. They said they would probably do interesting things, like work for NASA and look up exciting information about dark matter and dying supernovas. That sounded a bit, ummm sc-sc-scary, but maybe fascinating.

Me? I had first graders typing really, really slowly, and worse still, they typed the same words over and over and over again. It took seven minutes for the kids just to write the word, "cat." As you can see, my life felt slower than a slug's. I wished I were with middle school students because they type more quickly and learn about more interesting things. Once, an eighth grade buddy used me to look up information about "Big Ben."

In their defense, even the first graders seemed bored with typing on me. They said stuff like, "This is taking too long," and "My hands are starting to hurt," and "I would rather be playing four-square." I think four-square is a game where you try to keep the ball in your own square and quickly count to four.

After a few months, the class left for Thanksgiving break. At first, I was relieved to not be with those slowpokes, but soon, I began to panic. Were they coming back? Would I ever see anyone again? Would I be alone for the rest of my life? I had overheard Ms. Petunia giving a science lesson about the ocean once, and I imagined this is what it is like to be seaweed, floating out on open sea.

After about a week, everyone came back. I felt a bit silly that I had panicked. I realized that if no one was going to come back, they would not have left everything behind, like the posters, projectors, and Ms. Petunia's prized possession, a spike from the Statue of Liberty's crown that fell off, while she was sightseeing. In case you are wondering, it nearly hit her in the head, so they let her keep it.

That first day back, Ms. Petunia came and put her key next to me. It was a two-inch copper key, attached to a pyramid keychain that she got in Egypt.

Ms. Petunia said to her students, "Kids, over the break, I

went to Egypt. I went to King Tut's tomb and saw many tombs and hieroglyphics. As I leaned over to get a glimpse of the magical remains of King Tut, my key slowly slipped from my hand and fell onto his bones. I was afraid to touch them, plus there was a sign that said, 'Do Not Touch,' so I had to leave my key behind. I don't want to lose my spare key, so each day from now on, I will put it beside our computer."

After she left, the key suddenly said to me, "Hello, my name is KCK II."

I responded, "Hello, my name is TypePro."

KCK II said, "Do you want to know why I am 'II'?" Before I could respond, she went on, "So you may have heard that Ms. Petunia's first car key is with King Tut's remains, and I'm her spare key. Her last key was also named 'Kind Copper Key.' It's a funny story how she got that name. One day, the smoke alarm in Ms. Petunia's house went off. Lock-Up, her house key, was so scared that the house was going to burn down she screamed in a very high-pitched voice, 'I can't be a house

key if I don't have a house! I'm nothing without a house!' Lock-Up fainted and fell right onto her car key. Her car key soothed Lock-Up, saying, 'Don't panic. One time, I was going to the car wash and Ms. Petunia left the window open, and I thought I was a goner.' Her car key talked to Lock-Up, until she calmed down. Then they heard Ms. Petunia yell, 'I burnt the grilled cheese sandwiches! Noooooo!' Lock-Up said to the car key, 'Thank you for being so kind to me. You should be called

Kind Copper Key.' Since her original car key is with the bones now, I decided to keep the name, but since it's so long, I just go by 'KCK II.'

I asked her, "What is it like to be a car key? You must go on fun adventures in the car."

She said, "Yes, like this morning. We saw a bird poop on the car, so after school, we are going to the car wash again. Every time Ms. Petunia gets even a little bit of dirt on her car, she gets it cleaned because she thinks it's a fun adventure. The car wash has big gigantic brushes with soap on them. It sounds like an airplane when its engines are starting."

I told her how boring my life was and how the most exciting thing that happened to me was when Ms. Petunia bought me from the store. On the way to school, I saw large white flowers, lots of trees, and the calm, blue ocean. That's how I found out we lived in Hawaii. I thought my life would be grand, but instead, all I can see is one coconut tree outside the window. One time, I did see Ms. Petunia climb it to pick some coconuts for the students, which was pretty funny.

I asked KCK II if she could tell me about more adventures from her life.

Everyday, KCK II told me stories. One time, she said she got to see Ms. Petunia go to the bathroom.

"What's a bathroom?" I asked.

KCK II said, "Don't you know? There's a weird oval thing you sit on. Then you hear funny noises, and there's something called 'gas' that makes the funniest noise of all. It sounds like a brass band. Then there is some paper stuff that you use to wipe yourself, so basically you're wiping yourself with a tree. Then you press a button, and there's another loud noise, and everything disappears into a hole."

"That sounds so interesting! I wish I could watch someone go to the bathroom," I sighed.

After every story she told me, I sighed a long sigh.

Another time, KCK II saw a gigantic whale when Ms. Petunia was scuba diving. I thought it was kind of weird that she brought her key scuba diving, but she didn't want to lose it again. KCK II said it was very exciting, and a single tear ran down my screen. I told her how I longed to go on an adventure, but I had to stay in the classroom because Ms. Petunia didn't want me to get lost.

At that point, the bell rang, and all of the kids came back into the room. That's when Eliza sat down.

The Adventure Begins

Eliza was a first grader. She had long, dark hair, loved STEAM class, and enjoyed running really fast. She worked on the computer a lot. She didn't like to write because she said her hand got tired. KCK II and I noticed she was always nice to everyone, even the classroom technology. Some kids typed on me so hard, it was as if they were trying to crush rocks, but Eliza typed as light as a feather. She took very good care of me. However, she still did type reeeeeeeeally slowly.

One day, Eliza typed about cats. I was thinking about adventure, when I couldn't take it anymore, and yelled, "Can you type faster, and can you type about something interesting?"

Eliza was more startled than a deer in headlights. She asked nervously, "What do you want me to type about?"

I said, "Maybe King Tut or car washes." I yelled, "I am so bored!"

Then I started to cry.

Eliza told me she had an idea. She went up to Ms. Petunia and asked if she could take me home because she wanted to work on her report about cats and make a birthday card for her dad. She promised to take good care of me.

Ms. Petunia said, "Okay, but be careful!"

Joy filled my wires. For the rest of the day, KCK II prepared me by telling me about what I might see, like fish, sand, calm oceans, and coral.

At the end of the school day, Eliza put me in her bag. As she lifted me up, I felt something strange on my bottom and heard a "clink." She walked to her mom's blue car, which she called the "Zipping Blueberry." She put me in the back. As we were driving home, I heard KCK II's voice. She whispered, "I'm stuck to youuuuuu." The pyramid keychain was magnetic! I was so happy that she was with me.

When we got home, Eliza put the bag on the table. KCK II and I were still in the bag when a slimy, purplish-red nose stuck itself inside. We were both interested and nervous.

I asked KCK II, "Does it have teeth?"

We were wondering if it was going to eat us.

"Let's look up what this is. We can use you," said KCK II.

"No way! All I can do is have students type on me reeeeally slowly," I said.

KCK II said, "Don't be silly. You can do other stuff besides that. I've seen Ms. Petunia do it on her computer at home. She talks to someone inside named Siri."

I said, "Okay, well, I guess it's worth a try."

KCK II said, "Siri, what's the creature that has a slimy, purplish-red nose?"

I heard someone talk from inside me for the first time. I didn't know I could do magic!

Siri said, "It is a snarklewanger. It is an animal that has a slimy, purplish-reddish nose, a large mouth, lives on land, and can swim in water. It is the size of a small dog. They can run up to 450 miles per hour."

Suddenly, I had a bad thought. I yelled, "Do you think it eats computers and keys?"

KCK II became scared. "Wait, will it eat us? How do we

get out of here?"

I then asked, "Siri, what does a snarklewanger eat?"

Siri said, "Chocolate."

KCK II and I laughed. The snarklewanger laughed too. She introduced herself as "Slippy."

She said, "I also might eat the odd berry. My favorite is the crackleberry."

KCK II said, "A what?"

Slippy replied, "It is a slimy, greenish berry. You can tell it is not ripe when it is blue. But chocolate is what I really love. Sweet, savory, melt-in-your-mouth, delightfully scrumdiddlyumptious chocolate."

Then Eliza came back into the room. She pulled me out of the bag and said, "Oh no! Ms. Petunia is *not* going to be happy about this."

She picked up KCK II, who smiled and said, "Hey there!"

Eliza said, "Ahhhh, you can talk too?"

Slippy took this chance to say, "Howdy, Eliza!"

Eliza yelled, "You can talk?! That's impossible! Let me hear you one more time to make sure you can really talk."

Again, Slippy said, "Howdy!" and KCK II repeated, "Hey there!"

"Ooooo...kay? But I have to deliver you back to Ms. Petunia," said Eliza, as she picked up KCK II.

KCK II screamed, "No, don't. I want to stay with TypePro and see what adventures he goes on."

Eliza asked, "Who's TypePro?"

"You're looking right at him," KCK II said.

Eliza said, "The computer has a name?"

KCK II responded, "We all have names. I am KCK II."

Eliza said she had to call Ms. Petunia because she might be worried.

Eliza said, "Guess what? I have your key. It was stuck to the computer."

Ms. Petunia said, "I already got a ride home. Please bring my key back on Monday, Eliza. Just don't lose it. Bye!"

Molten Colten's Birthday

Eliza knew I had never been anywhere before, so she took me on a tour around the house.

She said, "Here's the bathroom."

"Oh," I said. "I've always wanted to see a bathroom."

We heard Eliza's mom yell, "Who are you talking to?"

Eliza said, "Just myself."

Her mom walked by us and looked at her strangely before saying, "You should know what a bathroom looks like."

After that, I tried to be quieter.

On Saturday, we focused on getting ready for Eliza's dad's birthday, which was the next day. His name was Colten, and she explained how he loved volcanoes. We watched Eliza bake him a cake. It was a chocolate cake that looked like a volcano. It looked so realistic with its streams of lava made from orangish-red frosting. It said, "Happy Birthday, Molten Colten!"

Eliza took us with her when she went to buy a gift for him. She decided to get him a volcano keychain. She got the idea from Ms. Petunia's pyramid keychain. The plan was to go on an adventure at Hawai'i Volcanoes National Park, even though he had already been there nearly a hundred times. Mauna Loa is the biggest volcano as well as his favorite, and his dream was to see it erupt someday. Eliza told us the good news. She would bring us too!

All night long, I could only think, "This is so exciting! Wait, am I going to get burnt like Ms. Petunia's grilled cheese sandwich? Should I stay in the comfy zone? No, I have to go! My wires are just longing to go on an adventure."

I looked up information about volcanoes.

The next morning, at 4:00 AM, we woke up to Colten yelling, "Wake-up, sleepyhead! *Explode* out of your bed. It's my birthday. I want to see an eruption today!"

Eliza yelled back, "Daddy, if there's a real eruption, we might die."

Her dad responded, "Don't fear, my dear. Molten Colten is here!"

Eliza, her dad, her mom, Slippy, KCK II, and I got into the "Zipping Blueberry" and zoomed off towards the park.

It took two hours to get there. Eliza put me in her backpack, so that I was sticking out of the top with KCK II's pyramid keychain stuck to me.

Everyone stopped to see a Hawaiian Lava Flow Cricket, when suddenly, it jumped on me. At first, I was startled. Then, I liked looking at it. It was brownish-green. We also saw craters and volcanic gases. It looked like a desert made of dried lava. It was so AMAZING!

We stopped to have lunch and eat the lava cake. We all started singing, "Happy Birthday," so Molten Colten could blow out his candles and make a wish.

Suddenly, the ground started to shake. It was an earthquake. The night before, I had read that after the shaking, there could be an eruption! Everyone started getting nervous, except of course for Molten Colten. He started jumping up and down with excitement, and he said he wanted to go closer. It was his birthday, so we listened to him. We were surprised to hear a big, gigantic rumbling sound. Then it stopped. Then it started again. It sounded like a train. Then there was a huge explosion of volcanic gases, pyroclastic rocks, and lava. It was hard to see and as hot as, well, lava.

Molten Colten yelled, "My wish came true! Now let's get out of here!"

He threw the lava cake into the lava and everyone turned to run away as fast as they could. As they were running, there was another earthquake. Eliza fell over, and when she did, I fell from her bag.

"HELP! HELP!" I screamed, but it was no use, they couldn't hear me.

The lava was closing in fast. They kept running away from me. Slippy happened to look back and saw me. By licking herself with her slimy tongue, she escaped from the hands of Eliza's mom and ran towards me like a flash of light at 450 miles per hour! In the blink of an eye, she picked me up in her mouth. I must tell you, it was strange being in the mouth of a snarklewanger, but I still gave a big sigh of relief. I decided right then to get Slippy a chocolate ice cream sundae, the size of a miniature pool.

Back to School

On Monday morning, Eliza's mom dropped us off at school in the "Zipping Blueberry." Ms. Petunia started to walk towards us. Eliza wondered, "Should I tell her that you almost melted in lava? Nah."

Ms. Petunia said, "Good morning! What did you do over the weekend? Oh, by the way, where's my key?"

Eliza gave her KCK II and said, "Well, I have to admit that things got a little hot for a bit, but overall it was good."

"Hmmm, maybe I could try letting students take the computer home every weekend," said Ms. Petunia.

That was the best idea ever! After that, I got to go home on the weekends with students. I realized that even though first graders are veeeeeeeeery slow typers, they are super at having fun. I went on roller coasters at amusement parks, climbed to the top of the tallest coconut tree, learned that kids pee in the ocean, and once nearly got eaten by a shark.

Now, for a change, I got to tell KCK II my adventures, and she was happy to hear them. Eliza was still the only human who knew we could talk. She spent a lot of time with us, practicing her typing. She got better and better and wrote about more interesting topics.

One day she decided to type a story about me, and that is the story you just read.

KARIANA EDRINGTON is an animal lover, a Mariana Trench researcher, a mathematician, and a reader. She goes to Cascade Canyon School. She has four people in her family. She has lots of friends, including her best friend, Norah. She is the author of *TypePro and the Terrifically Terrifying Adventure* and many more brilliant stories. She is one of the World's No. 2 storytellers.

Kariana Edrington has fun using made-up words, using magic, using talking animals as characters, and using adults as antagonists when she writes stories. She hopes her words will influence other children, motivating them to write creatively and imaginatively.

Project Reflection

My story is inspired by Roald Dahl in many ways. First, I made up my own words. In my story, I use "snarklewanger." In *The BFG*, Roald Dahl uses "frobscottle" and "fleshgoggled." Second, I use humor. In *The BFG*, the Big Friendly Giant farts because of the frobscottle. In my story, I use humor when the house key panics because she thinks the house is going to burn down when it is really just a burnt grilled cheese sandwich. To close, I tell a smaller story within the larger story. In *The Witches*, Grandmama tells Boy about the children who disappeared when she was a little girl. In my story, I have KCK II tell a story about seeing Ms. Petunia going to the bathroom. As you can see, my story is inspired by Roald Dahl in many ways.

Scarlet Rabineau

The vegetables

THE WORLD'S No.2 STORYTELLER

illustrated by Scarlet Rabineau

The Vegetables

Scarlet Rabineau

The Vegetables

illustrated by Scarlet Rabineau

This book is for my cousins, Finn and Max, who would love talking vegetables.

Hi, my name was... was... well, I didn't really have a name, but you can just call me, "Tomato." Anyway, I used to live in the fridge of Lucy Wiz in her family's house. My family lived in the fridge with me. My mom was Mrs. Snap Pea, my dad was Mr. Broccoli, and my little sister was Baby Avocado. The funny thing was that our neighbors had the same family. I mean, they had the same vegetables in their family.

One day at dinner time, the Wizzes announced that they were having salad with broccoli for dinner.

"Nooo!" we yelled.

Thankfully, but sadly, the Wizzes ate our neighbors instead.

"Do you think they'll make another salad soon?" I asked.

"I don't know," Mrs. Snapea said. "But, just in case, we should evacuate immediately!"

Eventually, we came up with a plan.  Here it is. First, we would wait for the Wizzes to leave the house. Then, we would get the cat, whose name was Bob, to open the fridge. Okay, I know this won't make sense to you, but we could talk to animals. After that, we would climb from the fridge to the window and open it. Then, we would run away to who knows where. Maybe New York? We got our plan in action right away.

My little sister loved my plan.

To show her excitement, Baby Avocado said, "A-goo, a-goo, a-goo!"

First, we called the cat, "Hey Bob, get over here! We need help opening the fridge."

"On it!" replied Bob.

He jumped on to the fridge. Then, on Bob's way down, he opened the fridge for us.

"Thanks," I said. "Now could you open the window, please?"

"Sure thing," said Bob.

Bob jumped up on the countertop and tried to open the window, but it was locked. OH NO! Just then, we heard a key turn the lock. DOUBLE OH NO!

"Quick," said Bob. "Hide behind the waffle iron and the coffee pot."

We did that *very* quickly. Just then, I came up with a plan.

"Bob," I said. "Could you run out of the house and down the street to distract your owners for us?"

"Of course!" he said, as he suddenly sprang into action and ran outside.

"Bob!" yelled the family.

I grinned. The Wizzes ran out of the house, chasing after their cat.

"Now," I said, "we just have to figure out how to get out of here before the family gets back."

"Well," Mrs. Snappea said, "they left the door open."

"Let's run," I said. "Follow me outside!"

"Where should we go now?" Mr. Broccoli asked.

All of a sudden, an idea came to me. First, we would go to the neighbor's house. Then, because somehow we knew that they had a son who didn't like eating vegetables, we could show him who we really are. After that, maybe with the kid's help, we could trick his parents into thinking that he was eating his vegetables.

Just then, we saw one of the neighbors come out of their house.

"Here's our chance," I said.

We ran for our lives and made it just in time. Then, we ran into what we thought what was Boy's room. Thankfully, it was.

We saw Boy for the first time. He was lying on his bed doing his homework.

"Hello," I said quietly.

"What, where, why, when, and how?" Boy exclaimed, as his math worksheets erupted from his bed and rained down upon us.

"Down here," I said.

"I don't believe my eyes," Boy said, flabbergasted.

"I know, this isn't something you see every day," I sympathized. "But I heard that you were smart," I said, trying to change the subject.

"Oh, I am. In fact, I'm going to boarding school tomorrow," he said.

"Wow," my family and I marvelled.

"I was thinking maybe you, my family, and I could all make a plan together," I suggested.

"What kind of plan?" Boy inquired.

"Well, we heard you don't like to eat vegetables, and I think I have a plan that could benefit all of us. When your parents ask you to eat your vegetables, you could bring us along. But instead of eating us, you could put us under the table or something like that," I said.

"That's brilliant!" he said.

"VEGETABLE TIME!" Boy's mom suddenly called out

from downstairs.

"Okay, everyone, this is *not* a drill! It's go time!" Mr. Broccoli said.

"Okay, coming!" Boy yelled back.

"Here!" Boy instructed, "Get in my pocket."

We climbed into his pocket and went downstairs, which didn't take nearly as long as when we travelled the steps on foot.

Once we got downstairs, Boy's mom said to him, "Oh, shoot. The phone is ringing, and I need to take this call. Can you cook the vegetables?"

"Sure," said Boy.

After Boy's mom left, Boy and I high-fived.

"Perfect!" we celebrated.

"But don't cook us," I said.

"I would never," he reassured us.

Then, he got a plate and put us on it.

Just then, his mom got off the phone and said, "Apparently, there's an emergency meeting at school. I'm afraid I have to go."

"Yes!" I thought to myself.

"But I'm leaving you here with your brother,"

"Oh no," I thought, concerned his brother may ruin our plan.

Once his mom left, Boy said, "Don't worry, my brother

isn't that strict about vegetables." He added, "Let's go upstairs. I need to finish packing, and it's almost bedtime."

The next morning, Boy got up and prepared to leave for boarding school.

"All ready to go?" his mom asked.

"Yep," Boy said.

"Okay, then, off we go!" replied his mom.

Oh, I forgot to mention that he brought us along, just in case someone there asked him to eat his veggies.

When we got there, his mom helped him get settled into his room. After she left, Boy introduced himself to his roommate, Jason. And as it turned out, he was strict about vegetables too. Good thing we planned for that! Or so I thought...

At dinner time, Jason said to Boy, "You should eat your vegetables. They're really good for you"

"Sure, but I'd prefer to eat the ones I brought from home," said Boy, as he pulled us out of his pocket and placed us gently on a plate.

"Excuse me for a second. I have to go to the bathroom," Boy said.

After Boy was in the bathroom, I heard Jason shake his head and mumble, "That crazy kid."

Seeing us sitting on Boy's plate, Jason looked ravenous. In one fell swoop, he grabbed us and ate us all up.

Jason quickly realized how rude it was to eat someone else's food, and as he waited for his new roommate to return to the table, he was hopeful Boy could forgive him for forgetting his manners.

SCARLET RABINEAU is a trapeze artist, a ukulelist, a receipt collector, and a pianist. She is the author of *The Vegetables* and many more brilliant stories. She is one of the World's No. 2 story tellers.

Scarlet Rabineau has fun using the title frame *The _____s*, using long e endings for her character names, using adults as antagonists, and using family members as characters when she writes stories. She hopes her words will influence other children, motivating them to write creatively and imaginatively.

Project Reflection

After reading Roald Dahl books, I learned a few ways I could improve my story writing. The first writing strategy of his that I use is humor. For example, in *The BFG*, Roald Dahl has the Big Friendly Giant drink frobscottle when he and Sophie are eating breakfast with the Queen of England. Another example of Roald Dahl's humor is in *Charlie and the Chocolate Factory*, when every kid with a Golden Ticket, except Charlie, wants to take something from the chocolate factory home with them. Veruca Salt wants an Oompa Loompa and even a squirrel! In my story, *The Vegetables*, it is funny when Mr. Broccoli says "Okay, everyone. This is *not* a drill! It's go time!" Another important thing I learned from Roald Dahl was using talking creatures as characters. In my story, I have talking veggies and a cat. *The Enormous Crocodile* has Trunky, the Enormous Crocodile, and the Notsobig Crocodile talking to each other as well as the children. Trunky says, "That's not a bench your sitting on! It's the Enormous Crocodile! And he wants to eat you all up!" In *The Giraffe and the Pelly and Me*, the Giraffe, the Pelly, and the Monkey all talk and sing. Last of all, I use tricks in my story, such as when Boy and the vegetable family trick Boy's mom into thinking he was actually eating his vegetables. In *The Twits*, Mr. Twit and Mrs. Twit play tricks on each other, like when Mrs. Twit puts worms into Mr. Twit's spaghetti. In *Esio Trot*, Mr. Hoppy tricks Ms. Silver into thinking that her turtle, Alfie, is growing. As you can see, my story is inspired by Roald Dahl in many ways!

Thea LaRoche

The Alphabet and the Giant

THE WORLD'S ★ No.2 ★ STORYTELLER

illustrated by Thea LaRoche

The Alphabet and the Giant

Thea LaRoche

The Alphabet and the Giant

illustrated by Thea LaRoche

This book is for my family -- my mom, my dad, and my brother Cole as well as my cousins.

There once was a letter, named G, who was loved by the entire alphabet, even though he was a "gassy genius."

One day, G decided he would go into the jungle. When he never returned, all the other letters assumed he had been eaten by the giant who lived there. The letters decided to catch the giant and lock it in the dungeon in the last room of their lighthouse, up on the fourth floor.

One night, during the witching hour, on the first floor of the lighthouse, the letter A woke up. She had heard something. It was a THUMP!

She looked where it was coming from. She saw two letters. It was B, who was brave, and T, who was known for being tasty.

These weird noises had never been a problem before. A was annoyed. The three of them looked where they coming from and saw another letter. It was named C, and she was the clever one. She had heard the noises too.

They all climbed up to the fourth floor of the lighthouse and tried to open the door, but soon remembered it was locked.

As you know, C was clever, so she knew how to unlock doors with a bobby pin. But when she tried, she failed.

A said, "I'll try it," and what do you know? She did it!

The dungeon was full of monsters -- some hairy

monsters, some monsters with one eye. T and A were scared and begged B to go inside first.

He said, "Okay, fine. I'll do it."

B went in but did not come out, so they all decided to go in, and they saw... B *and* the giant. They all ran out to make a plan.

1. B would jump out the window and turn into a boat.
2. T would jump out the window, land on B, and turn into a tasty taffy.
3. The giant would certainly follow T.

They ran back in and started work on their plan. First, B

jumped out the window and turned into a boat, and then T jumped out the window and landed on B. She quickly changed to a tasty taffy, just as planned.

But the giant did *not* follow T, so A jumped out the window to help by changing into an apple. But the giant *still* did not follow A.

It was all up to C now. She would turn into... a carrot? No, that wouldn't work. Giants don't eat vegetables.

She decided to add some carmel to A's apple. This time, the giant followed them all down and went splash! The giant drowned, and the letters thought it was the end, so they all cheered.

But then, the letters all noticed some strange bubbling and foaming in the water. Was it the giant? No, it wasn't the giant. It was... G? Wait, was he the giant that whole time? Would he ever turn into the giant again? And if he did, how would they stop him again? Who cares? It was party time!

THEA LAROCHE is a ukuleleist, an equestrian, a painter, and a ballet dancer. She loves her mother, father, and brother (sometimes). She goes to Cascade Canyon School. She is the author of *The Alphabet and the Giant* and many more brilliant stories. She is one of the World's No. 2 storytellers.

Thea LaRoche has fun using children as protagonists, having characters get eaten, using the title frame *The _____ and the _____*, and using magic when she writes stories. She hopes her words will influence other children, motivating them to write creatively and imaginatively.

Project Reflection

Writing a book like Roald Dahl is no easy task. First, I use monsters. In *The BFG*, there are nine man-eating giants. In my story, G turns into a giant. Next, I tell a smaller story inside of a larger story. In *The Witches*, Grandmama tells Boy stories about children mysteriously disappearing. In *Charlie and the Chocolate Factory*, Charlie's family reads from the newspaper. In my story, I write about G getting eaten. Last but not least, characters disappear all of a sudden. As I mentioned, in *The Witches*, kids disappear when they meet witches. One turns to stone, one turns into a sea creature, and one gets trapped into a painting. As you can see, my story is a lot like the Roald Dahl books we read in class this year.

Eva Mohtashem

The Fantastic Figure

THE WORLD'S No.2 STORYTELLER

illustrated by Eva Mohtashem

The Fantastic Figure

Eva

Mohtashem

The Fantastic Figure

illustrated by Eva Mohtashem

This book is for my cousins, Jacqueline and Olivia.

There once was a girl named Thea. She was usually brave, but she got scared sometimes too. Sadly, she had only one thing she was allowed to do at home, and that was knit in her bedroom. Thea had a very strict mom, who thought that this was a safe project for her. Thea didn't even know what to knit, so she hardly even did that.

It might seem like life could not be worse for Thea, but she had a mean teacher too, Ms. Hazell. Ms. Hazell never let Thea out to recess or lunch because she said that Thea talked too much in class. And to make matters worse, Ms. Hazell was Thea's NEIGHBOR!

Interestingly, Ms. Hazell had her very own forest with a giant tree that had a door. Thea heard that the door led to a magical place!

One day, on Thea's tenth birthday, she was thinking very hard on what to knit when Thea saw a figure in the corner of her eye.

"I know I'm not allowed to go outside," Thea thought, "but just this once, I'll leave the house to get some action in my life."

She started following the figure. As she followed the figure, Thea saw Ms. Hazell!

Before Thea could say hello, Ms. Hazell said, "What are you doing here, and why is my poor garden messed up?! It was you, wasn't it?! I have to talk to your mother about this. Stay right there!"

Ms. Hazell walked off toward Thea's house, so Thea continued off to go find the figure. She noticed that Ms. Hazell had apparently set a trap hanging from a tree. When you stood in the right spot, the trap would fall on you, and the trap was about to fall on Thea! But she ran out of the spot, just in the nick of time.

"Oh no! I lost the figure," she said.

As Thea was looking closely, she saw it heading toward the woods.

"Great!" she said to to herself.

She started following it again. When she was done and saw where the figure had led her, it was the door in Ms. Hazell's mysterious tree!

Thea had no choice, if she wanted to change her life. She had to go inside the tree.

She went in and saw a BIG party for her. It seemed like the figure Thea was following was her mom. Thea freaked out!

And guess who came through the door of the tree with her birthday cake? Ms. Hazell!

"But I thought you were mean?" Thea asked, confused.

"I was just trying to distract you to make for a better surprise," Ms. Hazell said.

"Well… thank you for doing all this for me and sharing your amazing and mysterious tree," Thea said.

"Why of course," Ms. Hazell said.

From that day forward, Thea had an amazing life.

EVA MOHTASHEM is an equestrian, a pet owner, a gymnast, and a mountain biker. She loves her parents, Karen and Mark, as well as her friends at Cascade Canyon School. She is the author of *The Fantastic Figure* and many more brilliant stories. She is one of the World's No. 2 storytellers.

Eva Mohtashem has fun using kids as protagonists, using alliteration in her titles, using adjectives in her titles, and using Mr. and Mrs. in her character names when she writes stories. She hopes her words will influence other children, motivating them to write creatively and imaginatively.

Project Reflection

My story is like a Roald Dahl story in three different ways. First of all, I have a mean teacher in my story. Her name is Ms. Hazell. She screams at Thea, always gets her in trouble, and never lets her out to recess. That is like in *Matilda*, when Matilda gets yelled at by "The Trunchbull." Next, I have strict parents in my story. They are like Billy's mom in *The Minpins*. She never lets him play in the forest near their house. In my story, Thea's mom only lets her knit. In *The Minpins*, Billy is only allowed to read and color inside. Finally, my protagonist, Thea, is a child. This makes it like *The BFG*. In that book, Sophie is the protagonist. In *Danny Champion of the World*, Danny is the protagonist. As you can see, my story is inspired by Roald Dahl.

Xander Lane

Holden and the Secret Plan

THE WORLD'S No.2 STORYTELLER

illustrated by Xander Lane

Holden and the Secret Plan

Xander Lane

Holden and the Secret Plan

illustrated by Xander Lane

This book is for my family -- my mom, Zoe; my dad, David; and my cat, Sven.

Once there was a boy, named Holden. He lived in a NORMAL apartment with his Grandpa Billy. Holden went to a NORMAL school, and he had NORMAL friends. For example, Holden played games like tag, and his apartment had things like a front door, a bedroom, and a bathroom. Although things were NORMAL for a while, things wouldn't stay that way for long.

One Saturday morning, Holden was making cereal for breakfast, but when he was going to get the milk on the other side of the kitchen, Holden stopped mid-step. Grandpa Billy had his head stuck in the newspaper, as usual. On the back of the paper, Holden read the headline, "Anniversary of Huge Peach on Empire State Building." Below that, it showed a picture of a boy who looked just like him!

Holden said, "Wow!"

Grandpa Billy said, "What is it?"

Holden stuttered, "Th-th-that boy on the newspaper!"

"Ohhh my!" said Grandpa Billy. "I thought for sure he'd be dead by now with those two mean aunts of his."

"What?" said Holden. "Do you know him or

something?"

"Well, yes, he's your twin brother," said Grandpa Billy.

"WHAT?" said Holden. "You never told me I had a twin!"

"Well, um, I have a history you don't know about," said Grandpa Billy. "I was married to your grandmother, Billana. Her maiden name was Trotter. We had three children together. Of course, you know we had your mother, Jane. We also had two mean daughters, named Sponge and Spiker. One very sad day, your mother was set up by her mean sisters, and Jane's car crashed. It k-k-killed her and your father, but at least, my two baby grandsons -- you and James -- survived. Shortly after that, your grandmother and I got divorced, and your grandmother got James, and I got you. You were little when all this happened, and I'm sure the car crash didn't make it any easier for you to remember. I am still so upset by the whole thing, I thought it would be easier not to share all of this with you. About a year after our divorce, your grandmother died, so James was sent to live with your aunts. Since I hadn't talked to any of them in so long, I couldn't do a thing about it. Who knows what they've told James? Probably some crazy story about your parents getting eaten by zoo animals!"

"OHHHH!" said Holden, "Can I go see him, please?" Holden begged.

"I guess," said Grandpa Billy, "but I've got to go to the the bathroom first."

Grandpa Billy was very old, and as you will soon see, he had to go to the bathroom quite a bit, and he was always reminding Holden to go to the bathroom too. After Grandpa Billy was done, they got in the car.

Holden worried, "Will James be nice? I mean, he's famous, so he has to be nice. Right? Will I be good enough for James?"

When the boy and his grandfather were there, there was a horribly long line.

When they finally got to the front, James said, "Well, how do you do? Do you want to hear my story?"

"N-n-no," said Holden.

"What?" asked James.

"I-I-I think we're long lost twins," said Holden.

"OOOH MY!" said James. "We have a lot of catching up to do. I suggest we go to my favorite vacation spot down in Mexico."

"I guess we could do that," said Grandpa Billy, "but first we'll all need to go to the bathroom."

When Grandpa Billy was finally done, they left in the plane for Mexico! When they got there, they immediately started catching up. James told him his story and what he had learned about Knids. James also told him about how he was asked to join Dahl Faction, the protector of all things good.

"Did you say yes?" asked Holden.

"Of course," said James. "Have you ever been on an adventure, Holden?"

"Well, my life is pretty boring," said Holden.

"Oh," said James.

"I really really want to go on an adventure. Will you help me?" asked Holden.

James thought about it for a moment and said, "No, you

could get hurt, and I just met you."

"WHAT, ARE YOU MY MOTHER OR SOMETHING?!" screamed Holden.

"Fine, fine," said James. "I found my adventure when a man gave me green crystals. He told me what to do with them. You'll probably find him near my old house in England," James told Holden.

Holden went back to the airport and got on the first plane to Aunt Sponge and Aunt Spiker's house.

When he got there, he heard noises inside. Holden peeked through a window. Was he dreaming?

What he saw sitting at the table was Aunt Sponge, Aunt Spiker, something fit James' description of a Knid, and something else that made Holden look twice. It had large pink rings around its nostrils. It was bald. Its feet were square, and in its eyes, he could see fire and ice dancing together. It had a mask and a wig sitting on the table next to it. Most disturbing of all, it was scratching madly at its horrible, disgusting bald head.

I overheard the Knid saying, "Our plan is to have the witch make mouse traps."

"I shall put a hypnotizing machine on them, so that the mice go into the traps," said the Witch.

"We will fund you, as long as there is no fruit involved whatsoever," said Aunt Sponge.

"Yes, and then we shall put Mouse Maker Formula 87 into candies. We shall kill the children and make the adults into our slaves," said Aunt Spiker.

"I shall have a giant pet mouse," said the Witch. "I already have the big potion."

"Let's go to my space station right away," said the Knid.

They left through a space portal, and Holden went inside the house.

He was hungry, so he grabbed a potato from the counter. The Witch had carelessly dropped something on their way out, so he picked that up too. He put it in his pocket with the potato. Holden then noticed there was still part of the space portal left, and it was disappearing second by second.

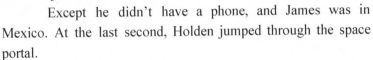

Holden thought, "Should I go in and save the world? Or wouldn't it be easier to just call James instead?"

Except he didn't have a phone, and James was in Mexico. At the last second, Holden jumped through the space portal.

When he got there, Holden saw a door. There was a robot standing in front of it.

"The New Society of Nice People are in a meeting right now. Please leave, or press '1' for more options. The exit is that way," said the robot, pointing.

"Okay," said Holden, pretending to leave.

When he was around the corner, Holden climbed into an air vent and crawled to a space, where he could spy on the meeting.

Suddenly the Witch said, "Stop! I smell dogs' droppings," as she pulled Holden out of the air vent.

What Holden did not know at that moment was that the thing he had grabbed was one of the Witch's potions, and it was now seeping into the potato. The potato suddenly grew larger and rolled over Aunt Sponge and Aunt Spiker!

The Witch exploded the giant potato with magic from

the tips of her fingers.

Just then James, Charlie, Sophie, and George blasted through the wall. It was Dahl Faction!

The Knid got so scared that it blasted an escape pod directly into a meteor.

The Witch said, "I was ready for you," as a cage fell onto Dahl Faction.

"I must do something," thought Holden.

Just then, Holden saw a mouse trap, so he activated it on the Witch's head.

After that, he freed them, and Dahl Faction and Grandpa Billy threw a party for him.

At the party, Holden asked James, "Is everyone here?"

"No," said James. "The man with the green crystals isn't here, Willy Wonka isn't here, and Roald Dahl isn't here."

Just then, there was a disturbance in the crowd, as Roald Dahl approached them. He snapped his fingers and turned into Willy Wonka. Then, he snapped his fingers again and turned into the man with the green crystals. He knighted Holden as the newest member of Dahl Faction!

Grandpa Billy was so proud of his two grandsons.

He said, "Just remember boys, being a real superhero means taking responsibility, and *that* means always being sure to use the bathroom before you start your next adventure!"

Holden was so happy that he wrote a book about his adventures, and that is the book you just finished reading.

XANDER LANE is a pet owner, a "Star Wars" enthusiast, a fiddler, and a drawer of stick figures. He goes to Cascade Canyon School in Fairfax, California. He is the author of *Holden and the Secret Plan* and many more brilliant stories. He is one of the World's No. 2 storytellers.

Xander Lane has fun using the title frame _____ *and the* _____, using children as protagonists, having family members die before stories begin, and using magic when he writes stories. He hopes his words will influence other children, motivating them to write creatively and imaginatively.

Three writing strategies I learned from Roald Dahl's work are borrowing his characters, having plot twists, and giving characters backstories, where they lose family members. My first Roald Dahl story strategy is borrowing characters from his books. I use James from *James and the Giant Peach* and Charlie from *Charlie and the Chocolate Factory*. In my story, James is a part of "Dahl Faction," and so is Charlie. Another thing I learned from reading Roald Dahl's stories is including plot twists. One of his twist endings is in *Danny Champion of the World*, when the pheasants wake up and escape from the carriage. Another twist ending is in *Charlie and the Chocolate Factory*, when Willy Wonka gives the factory, to Charlie. My story has a plot twist when Roald Dahl is revealed to be Willy Wonka and the man with the green crystals. Another very important thing my story has in common with Roald Dahl books is characters losing family before the story officially begins. This is like in *The BFG*, when Sophie's parents die, so she goes to live in the orphanage. Another example of a story where family members die before the story starts is *The Witches*, when Boy's parents die before the story, and he goes to live with Grandmama. In my story, Holden's parents die in a car accident before the story starts. As you can see, my story makes use of a lot of Roald Dahl strategies for writing stories.

Paloma Ybarra

Sammy and the Pet Store

THE WORLD'S No. 2 STORYTELLER

illustrated by Paloma Ybarra

Sammy and the Pet Store

Paloma Ybarra

Sammy and the Pet Store

illustrated by Paloma Ybarra

This book is for my family; my friends; and my favorite teacher,
Trevor Mattea.

Hey there! My name is Sammy Robinson, and I'm ten years old. I suppose my story all started when I had a dream about waking up on Christmas morning.

My mom said, "Sammy, come on down here!" "Okay!" I responded, as I dashed down the stairs and saw a huge wrapped box right in front of me. I asked my mom, "What is it?" She replied, "Open it, and you'll see." I ripped off the paper, and scraps fall all over the floor. "Whoa! It's so cute!" I exclaimed. My mom said, "I'm glad you like her." "We'll name the puppy, Fluff," I proclaimed. "What a great name!" my dad said in a proud voice.

When I woke up that morning, I got out of bed and dragged myself into the kitchen.

My mom was standing near the table, and I said sadly to her, "I really want a pet. Why won't you let me get a dog?"

I began crying.

"Sammy, please stop asking me that," my mom said, sounding annoyed.

"Well, then can I at least go to the pet store to look around?" I begged her. "Why do you hate pets anyway, Mom?"

"I used to have a dog, and I'll tell you, they aren't that smart. Ours went wild. He tore up all of my stuffies, ate my birthday cake, and attacked my little brother. Your uncle still has a scar on his left arm! You should ask him about it next time you see him."

"But mom! I know *my* dog would never do that. I'll train her so she behaves," I said.

My mom got even more annoyed and said, "I want you to be safe, and I want your room to be clean, so the answer is NO!"

"Well, then," I hesitated for a second. "If you won't let me get a dog, I'll just get my backpack, go and buy one myself with my allowance money, and move in with my friend, Lucy."

My mom responded, "I've seen tons of posters about missing children. I don't want you leaving the house."

I decided to ask my dad if *he* would let me get a dog. My dad is super lazy. All he does is watch football, and he pretty much agrees with whatever my mom and I ask him. If you are wondering why my dad is lazy, it's because my mom always pushes him around, and she said to him one day that she would take care of the house by herself, so he could just watch T.V. She also said that she would answer any questions I ask him. Anyway, my dad was sitting on the couch, as usual, watching television.

When I asked him if I could get a dog, he said, "Sammy, I have no clue whether or not that's a good idea. Have you asked your mom?"

"Then I guess I'm leaving!" I announced.

"Don't you want to watch the second half?" my dad asked, as I walked out of the room.

I grabbed my bike and rode down the hill to the pet store. I opened the door, and it went *ding* as I walked in. I saw so many adorable animals. I had never been inside a pet store before, and it was better than I could have even imagined.

I asked the pet store owner, "What are those two puppies named?"

"Ah, yes. Those two puppies are named 'Ruff' and 'Bone,'" he replied.

"Excuse me, mister," said another customer. "Can I please buy this cat?"

"Of course you can!" the pet store owner said.

The woman bought the cat and left.

"So sorry for the interruption," the pet store owner said, with a wink and a smile. "Would you like to meet the pups then?"

"Yes, please!" I said excitedly.

"Well, first you need the Pet Powder Potion," he said.

"Um, what's that?" I asked.

"You'll find out soon enough!" he said, as he sprinkled it on my head.

I suddenly felt like I was shrinking, squeezing, popping out fur, turning fuzzy, and getting very, very hungry! I looked down at my hands, but they weren't hands anymore, they were FURRY PAWS!

"Wait, have I turned into a puppy?!" I asked.

The pet store owner said, "Oh, yes, you did. You're a miserable little pup now," as he stared down at me.

"You can hear me talk?" I asked.

"Yes, I can. I turned you into a puppy, so I can sell you for more money."

"No! Ahhh!" I screamed, as he put me into the puppy cage.

"Bye-bye for now!" he said.

"Hey there! My name is Bone," said a white, fluffy puppy.

"And my name is Ruff," a little golden retriever added. "Bone and I are brother and sister."

"Uh, hi. My name's Sammy, and I'm not actually a puppy," I said.

"Oh, we know. We're not actually puppies either. We used to be kids too," said Bone.

Ruff said, "I like your name."

"Thank you," I said.

"We have some things we should tell you if you're going to hang out with us," they said.

"What?" I asked.

"Well, I always have tools with me," Bone said. "And Ruff is called 'Ruff' because he has rough fur."

"That's cool," I said. "But I think we should try to escape. Do either of you have any ideas?"

"Oh, I do! " said Bone. "We should rescue all the other animals. They were all once real kids, too."

Ruff said, "To do that, we'll have to get the Pet Powder Potion out of the office. That's the only thing that turns kids into pets and back to their normal selves."

"Let's do it!" I said. "Just tell me how to get out of here, and point me towards the office."

"We get out through this hole Bone made with her tools."

"And who says dogs aren't smart?" I said with a smile.

Ding! Another customer walked in the door.

"He's out now!" I said. "Okay, nobody run, we will sneak in there. Have you guys even seen an office before?"

"Well, not since we were actual kids, no," they said.

"Do you like donuts?" Ruff and Bone asked me.

"Uh, doesn't everybody? Why?" I asked, confused.

"Then let's dig into this donut!" they replied.

"Pups, let's focus! No donuts, okay? Wait, did you just eat one?" I asked.

"Numh, yum, chew.... uh, no, I didn't!" said Bone.

"Yes, you did," replied Ruff.

Bone argued, "No, *you* did!"

"We didn't eat any donuts," Ruff and Bone said, wiping the crumbs off their faces with their paws and looking very guilty.

"Look pups, we really need to get the Pet Powder Potion, and..." Sammy said.

"Sammy, watch out! Hide!" screamed the pups.

We jumped under the table.

"There he is," they whispered, as the pet store owner took a sip of his coffee before returning to the store.

"I have an idea," I said as we huddled up. "We should put the Pet Powder Potion in his coffee!"

"That's the best idea ever," Bone agreed.

"Then let's do it!" we cheered.

"Okay, on the count of three, let's dump it in his coffee, and say 'slug'!" I said.

"One, two, three, go! SLUG!" we all shouted.

"Here comes the owner now," I said. "Let's hide and watch what happens."

I heard a *thump, thump, thump*.

"Wow, he looks angry," I said.

Then a *sip, sip, sip*.

The room was silent for a moment. Suddenly, the pet store owner got on the table and started dancing around on his hands.

"It sure must be weird being him right now," I thought.

The pet store owner got down on the floor and started shrinking, twisting, turning into a slimy slug.

When he was completely changed into a slug, we grabbed the napkin from the donut, picked him up, and put him in the trash! After that, we grabbed the Pet Powder Potion and turned ourselves back.

"Okay, you guys, go get the other pets out of their cages and I'll put the Pet Powder Potion on them," I told them.

I dumped the whole bottle. After that, there weren't any more pets. There were just kids standing everywhere, crowded all around us, saying things like, "Oh, thank you so much!" and "We adore you so much!"

One of them asked, "What are your names?"

I said that mine was Sammy. Ruff said his name was really Alex, and Bone said her name was actually Scarlet!

We finally left, and all the other kids went back to their houses. I asked Scarlet and Alex if they would like to be friends.

"Of course! We couldn't have done this without your help!"

I walked through the front door of my house and apologized to my parents. I promised I would never, ever run away again.

They forgave me, and I told them all about what happened.

Finally, I asked, "Do you think I could have a pet dog now?"

Do you know what they said this time? They said yes! I was *so* happy, I nearly screamed!

After that, my mom and I went to a different pet store that only sold pets that weren't really kids, and we got a teacup pomeranian puppy. We brought it home with us and showed my dad the puppy.

I announced, "She will be named Fluff, just like in my dream."

After that, my mom helped me write a story all about what happened. Obviously, my dad was watching television. The story we wrote is the one that you just read.

PALOMA YBARRA is a gymnast, a hip-hop dancer, an artist, and a singer. She goes to Cascade Canyon School with her teacher, Trevor Mattea. She lives in Fairfax, California, with her mother and her cat, Nova. Her father lives in Los Angeles, California. She is the author of *Sammy and the Pet Store* and many more brilliant stories. She is one of the World's No. 2 storytellers.

Paloma Ybarra has fun making characters who leave their families, using children as protagonists, using the title frame _____ *and the* _____, and using magic when she writes stories. She hopes her words will influence other children, motivating them to write creatively and imaginatively.

Project Reflection

My story, *Sammy and the Pet Store*, is inspired by Roald Dahl in many ways. To begin, Roald Dahl consistently uses magic in *The Magic Finger*, when Girl uses her magic finger to turn the Gregg Family into ducks. Roald Dahl also uses magic in *George's Marvelous Medicine*, when George makes the medicine for his grandma. When she drinks it, she keeps growing and growing, sort of like a beanstalk. This is similar to the part of my story when Sammy sneaks into the office, gets the Pet Powder Potion, and puts it into the coffee. He uses magic in *Charlie and the Chocolate Factory* too, when candy grows out of the trees and everything is made out of candy. Most importantly, Roald Dahl uses talking animals in his stories, and I have done the same thing. He uses them in *The Witches*, when Boy gets turned into a mouse, who can still talk to other people. In my story, Sammy turns into a puppy and finds Ruff and Bone talking to her. He uses that device again in *The Enormous Crocodile*, when the Enormous Crocodile talks to the other animals. He even uses talking animals in *The Giraffe and the Pelly and Me*. Finally, Roald Dahl uses strict parents as characters many times, and I put some in my story too. He uses them in *The Minpins*, when Billy's mom does not allow him to leave his house. He did the same thing in *Matilda*. Her parents never let her read books, and they even tear up some of her books. They only ever watch television, just like the dad in my story. Sammy's parents never let her go to the pet store, so she leaves them behind. In *Danny Champion of the World*, Danny's dad initially forbids Danny from poaching because he wants him to be safe. As you can see, my story has a lot in common with Roald Dahl's books!

Matt Mulliken

The Jinx

★ THE WORLD'S ★ No. 2 ★ STORYTELLER ★

illustrated by Matt Mulliken

The J77

Matt Mulliken

The J77

illustrated by Matt Mulliken

This book is for my brother, William.

I am a chocolate chip cookie. My little sister is a brownie, my dad is a slice of chocolate cake, and my mom is a chocolate ice cream cone. My family used to live in a very famous refrigerator, right above a case of Coca Cola. We were really good friends with them. One day, as we realized our days were numbered, the Coke cans said that they would sacrifice themselves, so we would not get eaten.

One night after dinner, Dwayne "The Rock" Johnson was going to have us for dessert. When The Rock opened the door to the fridge, the drinks below us shook themselves up and exploded. This created a distraction, so we were able to escape. We ran for our lives. Soon we came to an open window, but we didn't know how to get out!

"How do we get out?" I asked.

"I don't know, Sweetie," said Mom.

We looked around for something we could use to get out the window when I found The Rock's step stool and showed my family.

As we climbed up the stepstool, The Rock said, "Hey, who took my yummy treats?"

He turned around and saw us climbing out the window and said, "Come back here!"

We got out the window and ran down the front steps. We ran out the front gate. The only problem now was that we were in the Hamptons, and we needed to get to New York City because we heard that humans were not allowed to eat much junk food there.

Luckily, The Rock lived right next to a bus station. We started our journey there. It felt like two hours for us because we were so small and getting around was hard for us. We hid and waited for the bus to come. Finally it came, and we were able to get in right before the door closed. We hid under one of the seats in the back row. I knew we were in New York City as soon as I saw the Statue of Liberty.

"Good news, we're in New York," I whispered.

We waited for everyone else to get off and then we snuck off of the bus. We ran across the sidewalk. Then I saw a taxi.

"Hey, we should take that taxi," I said.

"But how?" Dad asked.

"We need to get on top and grab onto the sign," I explained.

"Okay, let's do it," Dad said

It was hard to hold on, but we did it.

Fifteen minutes later, we arrived at a house. When the car door opened, guess who came out... The Rock!

"Ruuuunnnn!" I said.

We ran across the sidewalk for a little while. I told my family that we should go inside the next house we saw.

While The Rock was not looking, we went inside a house and hid under the couch. We stayed there for a whole year, until a baby came along and found our hiding spot.

"Ahhhhhhh!"

MATT MULLIKEN is a soccer player, a football lover, a pianist, and a video game enthusiast. He lives with his brother, mother, and father in Fairfax, California. He goes to Cascade Canyon School. He is the author of *The JFF* and many more brilliant stories. He is one of the World's No. 2 storytellers.

Matt Mulliken has fun using real-life famous people as characters, having his stories end with cliffhangers, using characters as narrators, and using family members as characters when he writes stories. He hopes his words will influence other children, motivating them to write creatively and imaginatively.

Project Reflection

My story is like Roald Dahl's stories in three important ways. Most important of all, my story involves chocolate. Roald Dahl was a chocolate monster. That means he really, really loved chocolate. His favorite chocolates were Kit Kats, Twix, and Rolos. In my story, the entire Junk Food Family is made of chocolate. Another important thing I learned from Roald Dahl's books was to have a child protagonist. In *Danny Champion of the World*, Danny is the protagonist, and I think he is eight years old. The protagonist in *The BFG* is Sophie, who is eight years old too. Girl is the protagonist in *The Magic Finger*, and she is school age as well. To close, I use real-life famous people. In *Charlie and the Great Glass Elevator*, the President of the United States is a character. There is the Queen of England in *The BFG*. In my story, The Rock, a famous actor, is the character who chases the Junk Food Family. As you can see, my story is inspired by Roald Dahl.

Joshua Levitt

Pander, Holden, and the Snake

THE WORLD'S ★No.2★ STORYTELLER

illustrated by Joshua Levitt

Pander, Holden, and the Snake

Joshua Levitt

Pander, Holden and the Snake

illustrated by Joshua Levitt

This book is for my family and friends.

Once there was a mole named Xander. He lived in Mole City, somewhere underneath the country of Mexico. Xander loved to hide. His favorite game was hide-and-seek. He was also very curious.

Xander had a friend named Holden. Xander and Holden met when they had a digging collision a couple of years earlier. Holden's favorite thing to do was dig holes. Holden's parents worked at a construction company.

Xander had always wanted to go above ground, but the law said that no kids under 15 were allowed to go above ground because of Joshua the Snake. You see, one time, a kid went above ground and got eaten by Joshua.

Joshua was a special snake because he was the last of his species. You knew when you saw him because he changed back and forth between blue and purple. People thought his purple and blue scales were poisonous.

Xander wanted to go above ground so badly, he could not stop thinking about it. Xander asked his parents if he could many times, but they always said it was too dangerous. They told him that if he went above ground, he could get eaten.

One night, Xander had a dream. In the dream, he was going above ground, using the last tunnel that still led up there. Nothing bad happened, until he saw the exit. Xander was almost there, when a purple and blue snake lunged at him. It was

Joshua! Then his dream suddenly ended.

Even if things went badly in his dream, he was still determined to go above ground. Xander went to his parents and asked one more time. His parents were working, so they didn't pay him much attention.

They said, "Sure, Honey, do whatever you like, but just make sure you're back for supper."

Xander started to dig to Holden's house. Xander asked Holden if he wanted to help.

Holden said, "What if our parents find out?"

Xander told him to do the same thing that he did, so Holden asked his parents when they were not paying much attention. They said yes too!

The two mole buddies started walking to the tunnel, when they saw a guard, standing watch.

The guard said in a deep voice, "Hello there, how old are you two?"

"Ten," they both said.

"You have to be at least fifteen years old to go up this tunnel," the guard replied.

They walked away, and Holden went to work digging a new hole to meet up with the tunnel that led out. They were about halfway through that tunnel, when we saw we were almost there. Then suddenly, a purple and blue snake jumped at them. It was Joshua!

They were in shock. They knew he usually stayed above ground. This meant only one thing. Joshua was trying to invade Mole City.

Holden and Xander ran back down the tunnel, and Joshua saw they were going to Mole City. If Joshua went down, he would certainly be captured. They saw Joshua stopped chasing them and decided to make a trap.

They told the guard their plan. They would hang a cage

at the top of the tunnel and put a special kind of rope, so that when Joshua stepped on it, the cage would fall on him.

The guard alerted the others, and they got cages and ropes, but then they said it would be too dangerous for Xander and Holden to help them anymore.

By now, Xander and Holden's parents were beginning to wonder where they were. They assumed they were just hiding and digging. They called each other to ask if they were at each other's houses. When both parents both said no, they all decided to look for them.

Holden and Xander snuck into Holden father's workshop. It was nighttime now, so it was hard to see. A guard was coming. They jumped into a tiny crane. Holden was not good at hiding, so he slipped and made a loud noise. The guard got inside the crane and looked around. Xander and Holden jumped under a seat. The guard did not see them, so he drove the crane out of the workshop.

The guards put up more cages, in case more snakes came. They were ready. Xander and Holden set up a trap at the main tunnel. Xander covered the crane in dirt, so it was hard to see. Xander and Holden dug a tiny hole and hid in it. Joshua was coming.

Down behind him, there were a lot more snakes, at least twenty. They came down ready to run. They started to run.

They ran and jumped over the rope. Joshua stopped before the rope and saw the trap.

"Oh no!" they both said.

Holden ran to get backup. Xander jumped into a hole that Holden dug before. Joshua did not see him.

Xander started thinking about what would happen when he returned home. He could get grounded, but Xander soon stopped thinking about it.

Xander jumped out and knocked Joshua into the rope. The cage fell over Joshua and trapped him.

Holden came with the guard. He was angry, but Xander did capture Joshua. The snakes were charging at them. They ran back.

Through the tunnel, the guards attacked the snakes. Then they saw Joshua, sneaking around them to the captivity center. Joshua escaped, and he was either going to release all the prisoners or eat them.

Xander, Holden, and the guard chased Joshua. The guard told them to stay behind.

Xander and Holden went to the crane, picked up a cage, and went to the captivity center.

Joshua threw the guard against the wall. Xander and Holden lifted the cage over Joshua. While he was distracted, Xander dropped the cage. It trapped Joshua. It was all over.

Joshua went to the captivity center, and Xander and Holden became famous.

Xander was still not able to go above ground, so he asked the guard to help him convince everyone to change the law.

When Xander finally went above ground, it was amazing. They even made a hide-and-seek park in his honor. It was all over the news. When he got home, his parents greeted him with a feast, and most importantly, moles of all ages were now allowed to go above ground.

JOSHUA LEVITT is a "Minecraft" gamer, a "Dungeons and Dragons" enthusiast, a gaga ball and tetherball player, and a pizza lover. His parents are Rachel and David, and his older brother is Daniel. He enjoys playing with his friends, Xander and Holden. He is the author of *Xander, Holden, and the Snake* and many more brilliant stories. He is one of the World's No. 2 storytellers.

Joshua Levitt has fun using talking animals as characters, using friends as characters, having the message of his stories be "work hard and never give up," and using magic when he writes stories. He hopes his words will influence other children, motivating them to write creatively and imaginatively.

Project Reflection

The three most important writing strategies I learned from Roald Dahl are making protagonists become famous, using child protagonists, and having the message be "work hard and never give up." First, in most of Roald Dahl stories, the protagonist becomes famous by the end. In my story, *Xander, Holden, and the Snake*, Xander and Holden become famous at the end. All the protagonists' problems are solved by the end of Roald Dahl's stories. For example, in *James and the Giant Peach*, James has a new, better home and friends. In *Xander, Holden and Snake*, Xander gets a hide-and-seek park above ground, and moles of all ages are allowed to go above ground. Next, my message is like the message in both *Charlie and the Chocolate Factory* and *James and the Giant Peach*. It is to "work hard and never give up." James works hard and never gives up. He thinks life was boring, but one day, he gets magic crystals and soon his life improves. In *Charlie and the Chocolate Factory*, Charlie never gives up on finding a Golden Ticket. It takes a while, but one day, he finds some money on the ground and buys a Wonka Bar with it, and it has a Golden Ticket inside! Xander and Holden never give up on capturing Joshua. Last of all, in lots of Roald Dahl's stories, there are child protagonists, mostly kids, who have older friends helping them. In *Danny Champion of the World*, Danny's dad and Danny go poaching in Hazell's Wood. In my story, the guard helps Xander and Holden. The child protagonist sometimes has to be sneaky and break the rules too. Danny sneaks in to Hazell's Wood, and Xander and Holden sneak into Holden's dad's workshop. Clearly, my story is inspired by Roald Dahl.

Holden Carr

Smokey and the Mysterious Disappearance

THE WORLD'S ★ No.2 ★ STORYTELLER

illustrated by Holden Carr

Smokey and the Mysterious Disappearance

Holden

Carr

Smokey and the Mysterious
Disappearance
illustrated by Holden Carr

This book is for my family.

Once there was a group of cats and dogs, who lived together in Norway. Anna was a little brown dog, who was great at finding food but also got herself into a lot of trouble. Xander was a dark brown cat as well as an excellent escape artist and all-around helpful cat. Alex was a black and white terrier, who always did research and made good plans. Finally, Smokey was a light brown cat, who was very brave. The four of them had been friends for a long time.

One winter, they decided that it was too cold to stay in Norway any longer, so they would take a vacation someplace warmer. After giving it lots of thought, they chose Mexico.

On the day they were scheduled to leave on their plane, Anna was picking up breakfast and got lost, causing the entire group to miss their flight. Since there were no more flights leaving Norway that day, they had to take a train to England and fly out from London instead.

Once they were safely in their seats aboard the train, Anna said, "I'm starving. How long before we get to England?"

"Exactly six hours," said Alex.

"Wow, that's longer than I thought!" said Anna. "I'm going to grab some food. Can I get you all anything?"

Smokey and Xander both said they would like to eat, but they were not sure what food was on the train.

Alex, on the other hand, replied, "I do! We have three

choices: Pizza, hamburgers, and chicken salad. I'll take a hamburger, please."

"Me too!" said Smokey.

"Well, I'd like a chicken salad," said Xander.

Anna responded, "In that case, I'll get two hamburgers, one chicken salad, and a pizza for me. I'll be back soon!"

After thirty minutes passed, Smokey, Xander, and Alex began to suspect Anna was probably lost again, so they had better go find her.

Smokey said, "I'll go look for her."

Xander replied, "I'll go with you."

Alex planned to stay behind, just in case Anna returned with their food.

Smokey and Xander looked all over the train, and after searching for another half hour, Xander finally said, "Where could she possibly be? Should we go back to our seats to see if she made it back?"

Smokey replied, "Alright, we can head back, but let's take our time just to make sure we don't miss anything."

When they finally made it back to their seats, they noticed that now Alex was gone as well.

"That's weird," said Xander. "What should we do?"

"Well, we definitely can't stop looking now," replied Smokey.

After searching for another half hour, Smokey and Xander noticed something moving outside one of the windows. Smokey went to get a closer look. It was a snake trying to detach the train cars, and they realized it was Joshua, the snake who tried to kill the President Turtle.

"We have to stop that snake! Xander, you hide, and I'll create a distraction. When Joshua is focused on me, you push him off the train," ordered Smokey.

Smokey jumped onto Joshua, and they wrestled for a few seconds. He tried to hit Joshua, but he missed. Instead, the snake bit Smokey hard in his belly, and he moaned in pain.

While Joshua was busy fighting Smokey, Xander popped out from his hiding place and tried to push Joshua off the train. He barely stayed on. Joshua then hit Xander. Smokey bit Joshua so hard that the snake jumped two feet into the air and nearly fell off. He was only hanging by his mouth. Smokey kicked him off.

Smokey and Xander then started to explore the train car that Joshua was trying to detach from the rest of the train. Inside, they found Anna, Alex, and other passengers tied up. They quickly freed the captive passengers. One of them was a doctor, who noticed Smokey's injury.

"Can I offer you some assistance?" asked the doctor.

"Yes, *please*. It hurts so much," replied Smokey.

It wasn't long after that that the train arrived in England. With all of the action on this ride, they were arriving over an hour late, and they would miss their flight yet again.

All the friends, except Anna, let out a loud groan.

"Shall we get something to eat then?" Anna asked.

"NO!" everyone else shouted in response.

HOLDEN CARR is a "Dungeons and Dragons" enthusiast, a gamer, a mohawk wearer, and a YouTube addict. He is the author of *Smokey and the Mysterious Disappearance* and many more brilliant stories. He is one of the World's No. 2 storytellers. Holden Carr has fun using talking animals as characters, using family members as characters, having happy endings, and having characters rescue each other when he writes stories. He hopes his words will influence other children, motivating them to write creatively and imaginatively.

Project Reflection

I did a few things in my writing that make it Roald Dahl's writing. First, my story is about animals who disappear. In *The BFG*, children disappear at night. Children in *The Witches* disappear too. Next, I have a character who likes to eat a lot. In *The Witches*, Bruno Jenkins likes to eat a lot. In *Charlie and the Chocolate Factory*, there is a fat boy, named Augustus Gloop, who gets a Golden Ticket. He has to leave Willy Wonka's chocolate factory early because he gets stuck in a pipe after drinking from the chocolate river there. Most of all, my story has a happy ending. In all of Roald Dahl's stories, there are happy endings. For example, in *The Twits*, the monkeys get free and the Twits get the dreaded shrinks. As you can probably see, my story is modeled on the work of Roald Dahl.

Zachary Looft

Pranks!

THE WORLD'S No. 2 STORYTELLER

illustrated by Zachary Looft

Pranks!

Zachary Looft

Pranks!

illustrated by Zachary Looft

This book is for my family.

I woke up like any other day. I had my regular breakfast of eggs and bacon with toast, and I engaged in my regular fitness regimen of a hundred jumping jacks. I played a game of Jumanji with my brother and roommate, Xander, and then walked to my job at the joke shop downtown.

On the way home from work that day, I noticed a new person moving into the apartment complex. He said his name was Jimmy. He seemed nice. I smiled at him, and he smiled back. He mentioned that he was in a rock band.

The next day, I woke up feeling groggy. I soon realized why. My new neighbor, Jimmy, had been playing music really LOUD! It was so loud, I could hear it from my room across the hall. Talk about an alarm clock! Well, what should I have expected with a rock musician moving here?

This started happening every day, and it was the most annoying thing I could imagine. I would wake up so early in the morning and get so sick that I couldn't even get out of the house. Xander left me chicken soup and then planned to go run the joke shop for me.

He said, "Who the heck is playing that music?! Is it that

neighbor again? That guy is so annoying! Why don't I get some stuff from the joke shop and teach this guy a lesson for you?"

"Umm... That is an ill-advised idea," I warned.

That afternoon, Xander said he got the stuff from the joke shop.

"I thought I told you I had reservations about this," I scolded.

"No, you didn't. You just said it was 'an ill-advised idea,'" Xander responded with a smile.

"Why don't you just talk to him?" I asked.

Xander replied, "Trust me, I did."

"Really? I'm actually not sure you did," I said.

"Trust me, he's as stubborn as a goat," Xander said.

We wrote down some ideas to get us started.

---

1. Tape a hand taser to Jimmy's door
2. Put super glue in Jimmy's soap bottle
3. Put banana peels through Jimmy's mail slot
4. Cut a hole in Jimmy's chair and put a snake inside

The next day was when I set up our first prank. I bought a box of a hundred fortune cookies and wrapped them in warm cloth. The moisture let me easily pull them apart. I took all the messages out and replaced them with messages, like "You will quiet down or we are coming for you." I put them into a big box and left them on his doorstep. Later that day, Jimmy opened up the box and ate the fortune cookies without opening them to read the messages. So much for that plan! On to the second idea...

That was to put baking soda and vinegar in Jimmy's pudding, so when he would take a bite, it would foam up and the results would just be disastrous! Unfortunately, it turned out that he didn't actually like pudding, so it was on to attempt number three...

We put a hand taser on Jimmy's door handle as we planned, and this time, he grabbed it like twenty times. You should've seen his face. It was like he was made of pure milk chocolate. So funny!

While I was laughing at him, I thought of another idea. Why not give Jimmy a popsicle made of snail slime?

Man! That was quick! Turns out Jimmy does not like popsicles either. Dang picky eater!

My fifth prank was probably my favorite. I cut a hole in Jimmy's chair, bought a snake, and put it under the cushion.

Sadly, the only snake they had at the pet store was a creepy purple and blue one, named Joshua. The pet store owner said he found him lying next to a train. Well, at least they had a snake.

On the way home, I got a chair, and at home I put the snake inside the chair and placed it outside his front door with a note that said "Jimmy" taped on top.

About an hour later, I heard Jimmy scream, "YOWSERS!"

Well, I did have at least one more prank idea from the list. It was called the "soap bottle super glue trick." We filled the super glue into one of our empty soap bottles we had lying around. We told Jimmy that we bought him new soap, and we covered the sides of it in dirt, so that when he grabbed it, his hands got all dirty right away. It worked like a charm!

That evening, Xander and I had a dinner party to celebrate when we heard knocking at our door. Xander opened it, but there was nothing there. Then I heard a little squeak and looked down.

There were two tiny moles that said, "According to the

laws of Mole City, we demand you give us that snake you stole."

"What snake?" I responded.

"Joshua the Snake, criminal mastermind, wanted for the assassination of President Turtle," the moles replied.

"I'm sorry, but I don't have Joshua anymore. He's next door with our neighbor, Jimmy," I told them.

Realizing this could be another chance to prank Jimmy, I suggested, "Well, why don't we sneak in on them then?"

"Thank you!" said the mole guards.

As we walked across the hall and knocked, Jimmy answered the door. He did not look happy.

"What do you want now?!" Jimmy screamed.

"I need the chair back." I said.

"Sorry, I put it in the dump and gave the snake back to the pet store," Jimmy responded.

The moles and I drove down to the pet store, and when we got there, the owner said that the snake had escaped. I heard a small scream and saw Joshua trying to eat one of the moles.

I grabbed Joshua's face and held it closed. The moles took me to Mole City, where we put Joshua in a fiberglass, soundproof box that hung over a lava pit.

While I was there, I was amazed by how beautiful it was. There was a park, an old workshop, and just what I needed -- a house for sale.

The next day, I bought the house, invited Xander to move in with me, and all was right with the world again, until there was a knock at the door...

ZACHARY LOOFT is a voice artist, a reader of many books, a sketcher, and an actor. He lives in San Anselmo, California, with his mother, father, and dog, Brook. He is a fan of Marvel movies, including "The Avengers," "Black Panther," "Age of Ultron," and "Doctor Strange." He is the author of *Pranks!* and many more brilliant stories. He is one of the World's No. 2 story tellers.

Zachary Looft has fun using dialogue, using cartoonish violence, using humor, and telling stories from the first-person point of view when he writes stories. He hopes his words will influence other children, motivating them to write creatively and imaginatively.

There are three things that my story has in common with Roald Dahl's stories. The first thing is using humor to show characters getting hurt, like in Roald Dahl's story, *The BFG*, when the Fleshlumpeater gets stabbed in the foot. In my story, *Pranks!*, Jimmy gets bitten in the butt by a snake. His hands also get glued together. The second way my story is like a Roald Dahl story is with its recurring characters. In *Danny Champion of the World*, Danny's dad tells him the story of the Big Friendly Giant, and the Roly Poly Bird is in both *The Twits* and *The Enormous Crocodile*. I have Joshua the Snake in my story, and so do Joshua and Holden. The third way my story is like a Roald Dahl book is that I use names from my real life. Roald Dahl uses his daughter's name, Sophie, in *The BFG*. He also uses his son's name, Alf, for the character, Alfie, in *Esio Trot*. I have friends named Joshua and Xander. My story, *Pranks!*, is similar to Roald Dahl's writing with its use of humor, recurring characters, and real-life inspirations for character names.

Ada Nichols

Dr. Tommy and the Tasmanian Trip

THE WORLD'S No. 2 STORYTELLER

illustrated by Ada Nichols

Dr. Tommy and the Tasmanian Trip

Ada

Nichols

Dr. Tommy and the Tasmanian Trip

illustrated by Ada Nichols

This book is for my cousin, Ruby; her dad, Jon; and her mom, Fay.

Hi, my name is Dr. Tommy. I lived in "The Town with No Snakes." You might be wondering why I lived there. Well, when I was little, a giant snake bit me, and it was *very* scary. I was terrified of snakes, not to mention dark caves, airplanes, and just about everything else. I also lived in the shadow of my brother, Albert Einstein. *He* was the one who invented the "Theory of Relativity." *He* was the one who came up with $E = mc^2$.

One morning, I was reading the *New York Times*, when I saw an article that said:

Calling All Scientists

125 bones found in Tasmania, but bone scientists there say they still need to find the last one. They are encouraging bone scientists all over the world to travel to the country to help in finding it.

I had a decision to make. I thought about the snakes and the airplanes, and then I thought about my chance to become the greatest bone scientist in the world. After a while, I decided that I would go.

I started packing my clothes, my toothbrush, a sack for the bones, and my teddy bear, just in case. I reserved an apartment in Tasmania, put my suitcase in the car, and drove to the airport.

After I went through security, I hesitated before boarding the plane. I stepped back for a moment, but I was able to pull myself together and take my seat.

Once the plane took off, it started to shake a lot. I was so scared that I peed in my pants. It was so embarrassing to ask for help changing my clothes.

When the plane had landed, I got off with my stuff. The flight crew handed me a trash bag with my dirty pants. As if I hadn't been embarrassed enough already, now I had to tote dirty pants all over Tasmania!

Once I got to my apartment, I went to bed to get a good night's sleep.

The next morning, I got up and started searching for the bone outside my apartment complex. There was nothing. I drove to the nearest park, looked for the bone for a while. Nothing there either. I drove to the nearest beach, and looked for the bone there, and I finally found a small trail that led to a cave. I saw the last bone far inside, but I knew that there might be... SNAKES!

Still, I really needed to get that bone and become famous. I didn't know what to do!

"It's only one little cave," I said to myself, trying not to think about the snakes, "so I'll go."

I started walking towards the cave, but I stopped before I went inside. I stepped back, but once again, I pulled myself together and went on. I saw something the shape of a snake... I went just a little bit closer and saw that it... Fortunately, it was nothing. I grabbed the bone and walked back out.

I said, "Now, it's time to go to the museum and become famous!"

I drove to the museum, and the people there helped me put the bone in a glass case for visitors to admire.

Just then, I saw Einstein walking in the halls, so I walked over to him and said, "Hey, Einy! How are you?"

He replied, "Great! How about you, Little Brother?"

"Awesome! Actually, I've never been better," I said, with a smile.

"Congrats on finding that bone, Bro! How did you do it?" asked Einstein.

"I don't know," I replied and shrugged my shoulders.

Einstein and I left the museum together and had a party with plenty of chocolate cake, streamers, and ice cream. We had a lot to celebrate.

ADA NICHOLS is an artist, a cat lover, a pianist, and a painter. She is the author of *Dr. Tommy and the Tasmanian Trip* and many more brilliant stories. She is one of the World's No. 2 storytellers.

Ada Nichols has fun using humor, using the title frame ___ *and the* ___, using alliteration, and having the message be "work hard and never give up" when she writes stories. She hopes her words will influence other children, motivating them to write creatively and imaginatively.

Writing a book like Roald Dahl is no easy task. First of all, I made some funny choices. In *The BFG*, the Queen of England drinks frobscottle and toots under the tablecloth. In my story, Dr. Tommy pees his pants because he is so scared of airplanes. In *The Twits*, Mrs. Twit puts worms in Mr. Twit's spaghetti, and Mr. Twit puts a frog in Mrs. Twit's bed. Next, I tried to model my title on those of Roald Dahl's books. I used alliteration by including "Tommy," "Tasmanian," and "trip," and "Tasmanian" describes "trip." In *George's Marvelous Medicine*, "marvelous" describes "medicine," and they both start with the letter M. Last but not least, I use famous people. In *The BFG*, there is the Queen of England, and in my story, Albert Einstein is a character. As you can see, my story is inspired by Roald Dahl in several ways.

Naya Thomas

Amelia the Dolphin

THE WORLD'S ★ No. 2 ★ STORYTELLER

illustrated by Naya Thomas

Amelia the Dolphin

Naya

Thomas

Amelia the Dolphin

illustrated by Naya Thomas

This book is for Eva.

Once there was a dolphin named Amelia. She lived with her mom and dad in the Atlantic Ocean off of the coast of Florida. Amelia was eight years old, and she was an only child. She felt lonely because she had nobody at home to play with.

One sad day, Amelia went to school and her fish classmates said, "You aren't a fish. You're a mammal. You're too big! You're not one of us! We only play with other fish."

Amelia felt very sad.

When she got home, her mom and dad said, "We'll be your friends."

But that did not cheer her up.

"You're my mom and dad. You can't be my friend," Amelia said.

Amelia wanted friends who were her own age. She went swimming into the dark ocean alone. Amelia saw a shadow. Suddenly, she felt scared!

Amelia said, "Hello? Please don't hurt me!"

She was shaking and whimpering. Then something came out, and it was a dolphin.

The dolphin said, "Hi, would you like to play with me?"

Amelia responded, "Sure, what's your name?"

The dolphin said, "My name's Estella."

The two of them swam away together. Amelia felt hopeful because she finally made a new friend. They started to play swimming tag.

While Amelia and Estella were playing they saw a big fish. They felt scared.

They said, "Oh no! A shark!"

They swam as fast as they could. The fish chased them.

The fish said, "I'm nice. Please give me a chance."

The fish caught up to them and asked to play.

"No! You're too scary!" shouted the dolphins.

The fish said, "My name is Roman. I know I have sharp teeth, but I'm not a shark! Please, I don't have any friends."

It reminded Amelia and Estella that they did not have friends before they met each other. They decided to give him a chance.

"Do you want to play with us?" asked Estella.

Roman said, "Sure, I'd love to play with you. What do you want to play?"

"We are playing swimming tag." said Estella.

"Oh, how do you play?" asked Roman.

"You swim as fast as you can. Then, when you tag someone, they're out."

While they were playing tag, Amelia asked Roman, "What's your favorite game to play?"

Roman replied, "Actually, I like playing swimming tag too!"

Next, they all saw a boat in the water above them. They went up and put their faces out of the water because they thought they saw something dangerous. They saw humans on the boat. They were afraid that the humans would capture them. Then they saw a cat.

They said, "Hi, what's your name?"

The cat said, "I'm Maya. How about you?"

Amelia said, "I'm Amelia, and this is Estella, and this is our new friend, Roman. We're afraid of the humans. What are they doing on the boat?"

Maya said, "The humans are just relaxing. They're nice. They're tired from spending a day at the beach and Disney World."

Amelia, Estella, and Roman were relieved.

"Can I sing you a song?" Maya asked.

The other animals said that they would love to hear her sing, so Maya sang them a song. The other animals told her that her singing sounded so pretty.

Amelia asked the three other animals if they wanted to have a party. Maya was feeling sad because she could not go into the water.

Amelia said, "Oh, but we can still have a party on the dock. That way we can include everyone."

They had a cake that Maya stole from her humans and watched the Disney World fireworks from far away. Maya sat on the dock, while everyone swam in the water nearby. They had so much fun together. Now they all felt very hopeful and excited to have a group of friends.

NAYA THOMAS is a pianist, a swimmer, a martial artist, and a doll enthusiast. She loves her mother and father. She is the author of *Amelia the Dolphin* and many more brilliant stories. She is one of the World's No. 2 storytellers.

Naya Thomas has fun using talking animals as characters, using family members as characters, and using names from her real life for characters when she writes stories. She hopes her words will influence other children, motivating them to write creatively and imaginatively.

Project Reflection

My story is inspired by Roald Dahl in three ways. First, I have animal characters who talk. All of the characters in my story can talk. Next, I take names from my real life. I had a friend named Amelia at my old school, Yick Wo Elementary School. Roman is another friend from that school. Last, I write about experiences from my real life. The characters make new friends, and I made new friends at Cascade Canyon School. Another experience from my real life is that I swim at the Bay Club and my characters, Amelia and Estella, play swimming tag. As you can see, my story is inspired by Roald Dahl.

TREVOR MATTEA is the editor of *O Brainy Book* as well as the second and third grade teacher at Cascade Canyon School. He previously taught at High Tech Elementary Chula Vista, a project-based school in San Diego, and Stevenson PACT Elementary School, a progressive school with parent participation in Silicon Valley. For the past five years, Trevor has consulted throughout the country to support teachers and administrators with  deeper learning, digital portfolios, project-based learning, parent engagement, and technology integration. He is also the host of the *New Books in Education* podcast as well as the former director of Imagineerz Learning, a Bay Area summer camp integrating social-emotional learning with making and design thinking. As an educator, his interests include supporting student-directed learning, fostering community, and sharing high-quality student work outside the classroom. He is a Google Certified Educator and Trainer and was recognized as the Silicon Valley CUE Outstanding Emerging Teacher in 2015. He holds an M.A. in Education from Stanford University and an A.B. in Political Science from Washington University in St. Louis. Learn more about his work on his website: **www.trevormattea.com**

Made in the USA
San Bernardino, CA
23 February 2019